THREE MISTAKES and a MONSTER

Plays by Geraldine McCaughrean

Illustrated by Belle Mellor

Contents

Pearson Australia
(a division of Pearson Australia Group Pty Ltd)
707 Collins Street, Melbourne, Victoria 3008
PO Box 23360, Melbourne, Victoria 8012
www.pearson.com.au

Text by Geraldine McCaughrean
Illustrated by Belle Mellor
Designed by Sara Rafferty

First published 2013 by Pearson Education Limited.
This edition first published 2016 by Pearson Australia Group Pty Ltd by arrangement with Pearson Education Limited.

2019 2018 2017 2016
10 9 8 7 6 5 4 3 2 1

ISBN 978 1 4886 1247 3

Pearson Australia Group Pty Ltd ABN 40 004 245 943

Printed in Australia by SOS Print+Media Group

Handmade Humans

Characters

Prometheus	a Titan
Zeus	a god
Hera	a goddess
Apollo	a god

Golden woman	played by the
Silver woman	same person
Bronze woman	
Woman	

Golden man	played by the
Silver man	same person
Bronze man	

Zeus, grumpy and uncomfortable, finds he's sitting on a thunderbolt and throws it aside. There is a moment's fun when it goes bang.

Zeus: Hera! Apollo!

Hera and Apollo drift in.

Hera: What is it?

Zeus: I'm bored.

Apollo: Why don't you zap something with a thunderbolt?

Zeus: I'm bored with thunderbolts.

Hera: You could triumph over some Titans. You know how you like triumphing.

Zeus: Yes. Send for Prometheus!

Enter Prometheus, defeated, enslaved, in chains, but dignified. The Olympians sneer at him.

Apollo: You could zap Prometheus with a thunderbolt, look!

Prometheus: Feel free. Before you conquered us, we Titans ruled sky, sea and land. What are we good for now? What use are we? Zap away.

Hera: You want to be useful? Right. Zeus is bored. Think of something to entertain him!

Prometheus seems about to refuse. Then he has an idea.

Prometheus: Oh, why don't you just ... invent some new creatures, Lord Zeus? Weak creatures, easy to bully. Creatures who do what they are told and who won't talk back.

Zeus: Hmm ... imagine that! Servants to wait on us! Fetch things ... do the gardening ... give us stuff ...

Apollo: What kind of stuff?

Zeus: They could make offerings. Give us food.

Hera: And flowers.

Apollo: And praise! Yes! Not a bad idea, Prometheus – for a Titan.

Prometheus: Thank you.

Zeus: You're right – we could use some worship around here. Prometheus, bring me gold!

Prometheus exits, then returns with a large lump of gold.

Prometheus: Your gold, Lord Zeus. Use it wisely!

Zeus zaps the gold. Enter Golden man and Golden woman.

Golden man: Look us over! Are we not the bee's knees?

Golden woman: Exquisite. Smooth, shiny and so ... refined. No, don't touch. You might leave finger marks.

Golden man: The colour of sunbeams, rustproof ...

Golden woman: And so pleasing on the eye, don't you think?

Golden man: God-like.

Apollo: What did he say?

Golden man: But who will hunt and cook and garden for us?

Golden woman: We must not get our golden hands dirty!

Golden man: Quite. And who will worship us?

Golden woman: The gods themselves, I expect.

Zeus, Hera and Apollo: WHAT?

Zeus: Take that!

A thunderbolt strikes Golden man and Golden woman and they turn back to gold.

Zeus: Far too uppity!

Apollo: But now who will serve us?

Zeus: Prometheus!

Prometheus: If at first you don't succeed, Lord Zeus ...

Zeus: But what shall I use?

Hera: Honestly, husband. If something needs doing, ask a goddess. Out of my way. I shall use silver. The colour of the moon. My worshippers shall be as lovely as moonbeams, you wait! Prometheus! Fetch my silver cloak!

Prometheus fetches her cloak.

Prometheus: Use it wisely, Lady Hera.

Hera: Insolent Titan. How dare you!

Hera lays the cloak over Golden man and Golden woman then removes it. Silver man and Silver woman rise and dance languidly.

Silver woman: Feel the peace!

Silver man: I feel it. I feel it. This place is totally peaceful, lady.

Silver woman: It's so blissful! Don't you just sense it?

Silver man yawns.

Silver man: I sense it. I sense it.

Silver woman: It's dreamy!

Silver man: Yes! But I'm really tired now ...

Silver woman: We should sleep. I'm beautiful when I'm asleep.

Silver man: You are. I am. We are ... beautiful.

Silver woman: Let's just lie back and dream ...

They sit down, lean against each other and nod off.

Apollo: What are they doing?

Hera: They seem to be asleep.

Prometheus: Why don't you wake them up?

Zeus: Yes! They have temples to build.

He hurls a thunderbolt.
Silver man and Silver woman sleep on.

Apollo: I don't know about you, but I'm not getting a lot out of this. Where are the offerings?

Hera: Where's the incense?

Zeus: Listen! Is that hymn singing?

Hera: Just snoring.

Zeus: Get rid of them! What use are worshippers who are never awake?

They roll Silver man and Silver woman offstage.

Apollo: Bronze. That's what you need to make anything useful. Bring me some bronze, Prometheus.

Prometheus exits, and returns with a large lump of bronze.

Prometheus: Very well. Bronze, Lord Apollo. Use it wisely.

Apollo touches it and Bronze man and Bronze woman burst onstage.

Bronze man: Right! Let's get to work.

Bronze woman: Yes. Time is money!

Zeus: This is better! Look at all the things they are making!

Hera: I don't know what they're for, but they look very ... useful.

Bronze woman is ticking off items on a list.

Bronze woman: Spades?

Bronze man: Check.

Bronze woman: Hoes?

Bronze man: Check.

Bronze woman: Chisels?

Bronze man: Check.

Apollo: Much better. Told you bronze was best!

Hera: Wonderful!

Bronze woman: Daggers? Shields? Spears?

Hera: Pardon?

Bronze man: Swords and clubs and axes and chariots ...

Zeus, Hera and Apollo: WHAT?

Bronze man: And hammers.

Bronze woman: No, tongs.

Bronze man: Hammers.

Bronze woman: Tongs.

Suddenly, Bronze man and Bronze woman are arguing.

Bronze man: Hammers!

Bronze woman: Tongs!

Bronze man: Hammers!

Bronze woman: Tongs!

Zeus has his fingers in his ears.

Zeus: STOP !

Zeus zaps Bronze man and Bronze woman with a thunderbolt. They lie curled up on the stage.

Zeus: Well, that was a disaster!

Long, embarrassed pause.

Prometheus: I have a suggestion ...

Hera: You, Prometheus? Haven't you done enough harm?

Prometheus: It's just ... I'm a sculptor, Lord Zeus. I could make you some worshippers ...

Apollo: Ha! You're only a Titan – making creatures is gods' work!

Zeus: Quiet, Apollo! Let him try. It can't be worse than your effort. Do it!

Prometheus: Very good, Lord Zeus.

Hera: What's he doing, squatting in the dirt like that?

Apollo: He's never going to make them out of mud!

Hera: Ugh. Typical Titan. Olympians would never dirty their hands!

Prometheus uncurls man and woman, who are holding a baby. Prometheus whispers to them as he works.

Prometheus: Iron for your bones and
clay for your flesh;
I make you with love, and
I make you the best.
Delicate fingers and
feelings and face;
Courage and stamina,
sweetness and grace.
Secretly, people,
between you and me,
They call you slaves,
but I've made you FREE.

Prometheus turns to Zeus.

Your people are ready, Lord Zeus.

Zeus: Off you go, then, Titan. ... Wait. What did you call them?

Prometheus: 'People', Lord Zeus.

Zeus: Silly name. ... All right, all right, get out.

Apollo: They're quite stupid, these ... er ... poople.

Hera: And ugly.

Zeus hurls a thunderbolt.

Zeus: But very easy to scare.

Apollo: And eager to please.

Hera: And – oooh – listen. They can sing!

Woman is singing to a baby cradled in her arms.

Woman: Go to sleep, my little one ...

Prometheus enters and speaks to the audience.

Prometheus: In time, every hill and shore and plain will bear my people's footprints. Long after the gods have grown old and feeble, Humankind will clamber about the planet clinging on as best it can. I mean to help them – oh, not out of hate for the Olympians. Revenge is a fool's game. No. I shall help them out of love. Because I made them. They are my ... children.

Apollo: Oh no – that baby's crying!

Hera: These 'poople' make such a racket!

Zeus: Are you sure this was a good idea of yours, Prometheus? Ah well, they don't live forever, I suppose.

Exit the gods with their fingers over their ears.

The Riddle of the Sphinx

Characters

Showoff *and* **Traveller**	Hoping for fame and riches, with his fingers firmly crossed. Accepts whatever life brings. Nothing much surprises him.
Sphinx	A monster with the body of a lion and the head of a beautiful, unhappy woman.
Queen Jocasta	Queen of Thebes
Prime Minister *and* **A citizen**	Honourable and brave, wants to protect the queen from sorrow.
Gawper	Likes watching but won't take risks.
Chancer *and* **A citizen**	A woman, more hungry than ambitious.

A road outside Thebes. It is patrolled by the sphinx. At a safe distance, a crowd has gathered.

Showoff: Look at the size of her!

Gawper: She's been prowling the road for weeks! Asking hcr stupid question.

Chancer: No one can get into Thebes, and no one can get out. We're running out of food!

Gawper: That monster has besieged us. Somebody do something!

Showoff: Yes, someone needs to put a stop to this. I'd do it myself, only …

Chancer: Shh … Look! Here comes the queen!

Enter Queen Jocasta with Prime Minister.

Prime Minister: Silence, citizens. Queen Jocasta wishes to speak.

Queen Jocasta: My people! We are living in desperate times. This monster, the sphinx, is like a curse on our city. Even our greatest general has failed to drive her away – tried and failed, and died – like all the others who went before him.

Prime Minister: And so the queen, in her wisdom, issues this proclamation. Whoever answers the Riddle of the Sphinx shall be King of Thebes, and shall have her royal hand in marriage.

Gawper: King of Thebes, eh?

Showoff: My big chance! Make way, world, for the next King of Thebes.

Showoff turns to Chancer.

Showoff: Look at you, scaredy cat. You'll never rule a kingdom! But I will! I mean, how hard can it be? Riddles are party games. Any child can solve a riddle. King of Thebes. That suits me.

Gawper: I think I'll just stay here and watch.

Showoff goes up to Sphinx. Sphinx roars.

Sphinx: Halt and answer! Live or die! What has four legs in the morning, two at noon, three in the evening, and is weakest when it has the most?

Showoff: Easy! A constellation in the sky – one of the signs of the zodiac, you know? Though I'm not sure **which** exactly ...

Sphinx: Wrong, mortal! Now I shall tell you another and answer it myself. What bed does no man climb into, no man climb out of and yet all men lie in?

Showoff: I …

Sphinx: HIS GRAVE!

There is a sound of terrible roaring. Showoff backs off, screaming, chased by Sphinx.

Prime Minister: Another life lost, Your Majesty. The sphinx is pitiless.

Queen Jocasta: I fear you are right, Prime Minister. But the gods will help! Someone will save us! Surely!

Gawper: Don't look at me! Here's someone, though. Here comes another chancer.

He calls to Chancer.

Do you think the queen will let a **woman** be King of Thebes?

Chancer: Maybe we can take it in turns to be Queen. Never mind the reward. Look at it this way – I can sit here and starve, or risk it and maybe taste food again before I die. How hard can it be to solve a silly riddle?

Gawper: I think I'll just stay here and watch.

Sphinx enters. Chancer goes up to her. Sphinx roars.

Sphinx: Halt and answer! Live or die! What has four legs in the morning, two at noon, three in the evening, and is weakest when it has the most?

Chancer: Four, two, three. Give me a minute. I'll get there. One woman to another ... give me a clue. Is it animal, vegetable or mineral? A tree! A squid. One of the gods! A sphinx!

Sphinx: Enough, mortal! You have failed. I shall tell you another and answer it myself. Everyone walks towards me while wanting me farther off. What am I?

Chancer: I …

Sphinx: DEATH!

There is a terrible roar, and Chancer runs offstage, followed by Sphinx. There is a pause. Sphinx re-enters, alone.

Gawper: If I say what I saw here today, no one else will ever volunteer.

Queen Jocasta: No one else is willing? Not one?

Prime Minister: It is a terrible way to die, Your Majesty.

Queen Jocasta: Yes – it is terrible indeed to be torn into pieces by a monstrous lion with wings that blot out the sun. Perhaps the sphinx is a queen, like me. Perhaps it will take a queen to answer the riddle.

Prime Minister: I beg you not to try. It is utterly impossible. So many have guessed. So many have died.

Queen Jocasta: You are right. I am not wise enough.

She thinks.

But you are, Prime Minister. The wisest man in Thebes. I have always said so.

Prime Minister: Thank you, Your …

Realising what she means, he falters, then bows.

Prime Minister: I will serve Thebes with my last breath, Your Majesty.

The Prime Minister approaches the sphinx. The queen whispers to herself.

Queen Jocasta: Thank you, dear Prime Minister.

Sphinx roars.

Sphinx: Halt and answer! Live or die! What has four legs in the morning, two at noon, three in the evening,and is weakest when it has the most?

Gawper: I can't watch. I can't. I won't.

He watches.

Prime Minister: Before I answer, **I** have questions for **you** to answer. Why Thebes? Did we anger the gods? Why the sadness in your face? Why the anger in your heart?

Sphinx: What has four legs in the morning, two at noon, three in the evening, and is weakest when it has most?

Prime Minister: I do not know! I do not care. Do you? I don't believe you even know why you are asking it or what you are doing here, day after day.
I love life. But I refuse to fear death.
How about you? Come on. It's not a riddle. It's a simple question.

He does not run. Sphinx drags him offstage, roaring, then re-enters crying.

Enter Traveller, limping, with a crutch.

Monstrous roaring and howling from Sphinx.

Sphinx: Halt and answer! Live or die!
What has four legs in the …

Traveller: Were you crying just then?

Sphinx: What has four legs in the morning, two at noon, three in the evening and is weakest when it has most?

Traveller: And good morning to you too.
Are you local? Can you tell me – is this the road to Thebes?

Sphinx rears up to kill Traveller.

Traveller: All right, all right. Keep your fur on. What has four legs in the morning, two at noon and three in the evening? That old chestnut? **We do**, of course. Everyone knows that. As a baby we crawl. As grown adults we walk on two legs. In old age we lean on a stick ... Though me, of course – I've leaned on a stick all my life. It's my feet, you know. Wait! Don't upset yourself.

Sphinx: Where one wins, the other must lose.
You have won your life, mortal!
It follows that I must lose mine …

Sphinx rushes off with a terrible scream of rage and despair.

The traveller watches in horror.

Various citizens crowd on stage, pull him to his feet and congratulate him. As he recounts what happened, the queen enters.

Traveller: She just threw herself into the ravine!
Didn't even spread her wings.
Terrible!

Gawper: We saw! But weren't you scared?
We saw you! You solved the riddle!

Queen Jocasta: Yes, the sphinx besieged the city,
cut us off from the outside world,
killed every traveller on the road!
Everyone but you … er …

Traveller: Me? Oh. Just a traveller.

Queen Jocasta: I kiss your feet, Traveller. You have saved my city and won the crown. Take me too, for your queen.

Citizens: Lucky man!

Gawper: I wish I'd had a go at guessing. That could have been me!

Traveller: It sounds like a sweet fate, lady. And a man should not run from Fate. Let me try the words on for size – "King of Thebes". Do they suit me?

Rest of cast: Hail, King of Thebes!